KINTSUGI

FLOOD EDITIONS

KINTSUGI

THOMAS MEYER

Published by Flood Editions

www.floodeditions.com

ISBN 978-0-9819520-9-3

Cover photograph by Reuben Cox

Design and composition by Quemadura

Printed on acid-free, recycled paper

in the United States of America

This book was made possible in part through

a grant from the Illinois Arts Council

FOREWORD

In that sad and famous way in which every photograph is, whatever else it is, somehow also about pastness—itself the quality that Wittgenstein felt epitomized by a certain passage, "As if from far away," in Schumann's *Dances for the David Brotherhood* —in some kindred way we can and perhaps should read every poem as an elegy.

In Homer grieving for the men of old who mourned for Linos, in Virgil's meaty grieving for the very substance or flesh he gazed at, fleeting as its perception, we read that sorrow which is the true ground of language. It is the reference that language, in its essence and by its presumed first purpose, makes *to what is not here*. Every object or relationship or feeling, ill-roused from its sleep by words, soon slips back into lostness, pastness, leaving the same sort of aftertaste that music does.

I don't think I ever felt this more keenly than when I read Tom Meyer's elegy for Jonathan Williams, his partner of nearly four decades, a text written in and through the very death it mourned —like a parallel text to that dying. The ancients used to speak of one who is in the very act of dying as being *in articulo mortis*, the limb of it, in the nick of death.

Tom calls the threnodic pulses of his observation of Jonathan's dying, his own surviving, by a curious Japanese word, *kintsugi*, which he describes as the "practice of repairing ceramics with gold-laced lacquer to illuminate the breakage." So the very rupture is what is highlighted: the error becomes the meaning of the text. Tom's *presence* to the dying and the death and the after is the golden line that holds all this together. His love that is so worn and deep and thorough that it does not need to speak its usual endearments. When we are that close, so close that the whole of one's attention is given to that person who is going away, love means little more than paying attention. In a strange, almost selfish way, the reader (or this reader) feels embraced too a little in the amative circle of that attention, his own secret breaks and fissures healed by these lines sung at right angles to us, and straight at the dying man.

ROBERT KELLY

X

KINTSUGI: JAPANESE PRACTICE
OF REPAIRING CERAMICS
WITH GOLD-LACED LACQUER TO
ILLUMINATE THE BREAKAGE

FORTY-EIGHT PIECES

All dogs bark his name.
He who has gone

there from here
past time's gap. Jumped.

Do we come back in our fathers' blood?
What happened a year ago gets pierced by today?

Where did I leave that book? In the car.
Those uncertain seconds are everything

when I can't put my hand on it
whatever it is. Or wherever.

A new moon. What is not there felt for.
In the dark. Get up, go out to the car.

Set the chair at the table and put
the loaf right there. No knife. Tear it.

Sit. Write. I drift. Books. In black and white
the honey here of a difficult pattern not
to shy from or even follow but let stand
until it sticks. Is that all there is? Some
lines going where.

A place the tongue finds. An afternoon.
Tasted. Said. All the world Mayan

while here we are to wonder: Is this seen?
Or heard. Herd. Scene.

4

At the frilly edges of thinking. Such.
Thoughts.

Sit so you don't hurt the grass.
An impossible grace

everyday we
fall from.

To sit while outside a light but steady rain falls
while someone walks into the room
though he's not there if I look up. I won't.

What a luxury this loneliness is.
To sit in the sun on that flat spot
up behind the house
where the bloodroot still hasn't come
to tell me you are gone.

Once a river only a shudder
of sunlight and water is left

and a complete blank
when it comes to deserts.

Drought I've seen though
how the sight of no rain

looks remains, not a mystery,
but another cul-de-sac

talking about it leads us
down.

That shelter included shadow, surprises.
But why? Hidden under a bushel basket.
Stood in front of. Protection.

Each hand cupped and whatever it is
that needs this care slips like water
through the fingers but remains refreshment.

The key is here but not the room number.
Does that mean try all the locks?

Or wait? For what? I'm sure any angel
would agree: Who wants in when the time comes?
Not the time, but Time. Who, just who.

In a pool beside the sycamore
we see who hides in that tree

with a hand to cup cold water.
Who will come down when?

Careful of the stars when you pass
through the cloud. At the edge of town

I'm standing there. Then look up. See
you and me on a sled

in each other's arms sliding down
a slope. New snow.

What disturbs the air? Strikes the note
and breaks the cord? A match
struck in the dark, after it goes out,
after a few minutes the eye can see
full well.

You whom I never dream of I dream of
your tender final sleep
and think of

those kids lost in the woods
praying to a sonnet of angels
to protect them:

Go, my envoy, into
the month spring comes.

Gathered up and let go. Honeysuckle, wisteria.
A river of stars. Hold my hand.

Startled rust, black and white towhee on the gravel.
Slow long cool spring. Red fox

carries the gingerbread boy across the river. Run
for your life. Run.

My feet almost not there in the wet grass.
An evening, not cold yet spring.

It has come to this.
My sitting here writing this
beside your sleep.

Pindar had it right:
Sing for those

who hear the song
and they . . .

what?
Last. Their souls

asleep, limbs
awake.

10

A thief in the night. Did I say that already?
But isn't everything in the dark stolen?
Day's other half the great burglar
of all we hold on to then let go of.

Gap you could drive a Mack truck through
or the whole vernacular.

Then what's left?
Apart from a personal indifference to pronouns.

All my life I've been waiting for something
and now here it is. Unapparent

like a wood in Germany. Not fog but a mist
for a moment obscures you.

An empty pair of shoes out in the middle of the room.
The thing about waiting. Take away anticipation
and that's all there is. Those words from Latin
"I" tries to avoid. A lesson I can't or it won't be
learned.

Talk with us. We too fear both fire and time
certain they are the same. What is left
when they are done? What is left to do
but move to Spain and live there life's cruelty.

Walk into a room.
Not know where I am.
Once it was Love
had me so distracted.
Now it's Death.

It won't be hours until this happens
what took seconds to transpire.

Moments in each other's arms
when time is a toy. Something simple.

Winds up. Runs down. Clatters.

The story itself isn't remarkable
though not all that believable:

a young man, apparently the gardener,
who tells the women to do something

they don't and then they run away afraid.

.

It hardly matters. I've probably already heard it.
Or never will. Anticipation is the—what to call it?
Not the "answer," really.

There is a music
I've been waiting for
I want to say
all my life.

Some vast Russian novel in which I am packing
and unpacking belongings. Mine? I own? My Hindu friends
tell me I'm part of a long line of warriors but
in this life a writer under Saraswati's blessing.

Flesh and grass. Brahms' Requiem.
The women weep over the last lines.
The ones not written yet.

They carry a child.

Forty-some years ago
he would've been the Aeon. Today
he sells cars south of Chicago.

I often mistake the watering can for the cat.
For that matter any flux of shadow
seems to be him coming to find me.

"In the middle of the floor," I wanted to say.
Or meant, but it was an emptiness that swept
away that ground to include what else?
Windows? Chairs? A table. A "where,"
and a "we are ..."

Who must dream the dream
before we can dance it?
Honey in the difficult
pattern of dark and light.

That world we see
is music, music in a dream then.

It moves. Red sun. Green field.
Black angus. Tree above.

Rain. Or night.
Ever careful of the stars.

Yellow river. In a distant haze klezmer music.
On those banks pamplemousse was invented.

No time for Chinese philosophy. One foot
in front of another. "Not being there."

For that they drew a branch to show
the bird had flown.

Put the ending on the table.
Better yet, in the drawer.

Forget beginning and middle.
They are lies. Neither has been

nor ever was. Where were they?
This is the happiness that wipes

the face clean and puts a smile
on it. Stars in your eyes.

Napoleon's men didn't want to
(or couldn't) restore the rose's petals
to the diadem of its stem.

Forever water falls. An ankle held between neck and shoulder.
Completely but easily. Someone walking in the hallway.
Morning details swept up. A damp sheet pulled out from under
    a hip.
Something. Or rather some place. Fingers discover.

Not quietude, but reticence. What does that mean? A net?
A tacit agreement. Again. Not saying. Not saying. Again.

A car though the leaves barely seen
except for sunlight on a wet
morning.

A fight to get rid of "like." Not even
"A car ..." Movement. Something.
Color.

Then something else steps in:
"though the leaves barely seen
except."

For me the hardest and last things to do
have been the least.

18

To pick up your glasses and know
you will never look through them again.

La vita nuova. Where does it end.
Or begin when. The rain and wind were
only mice in the ceiling. Mice

in the silence. Lips parted, slight arch
of tongue. A bit of air.

There was a book there before I nodded off
my hand can't find nor is there enough light
to see just where I am. A place I know I knew
yet can't quite place right now.

The curtain lifts and the dead enter
while the living exit. This is what the world is.
A hand held out amidst noise and dust
whose touch is a wide-eyed lifetime.

No end to what is, and not water
or whatever else we know as stuff

all that comes from this. While everything
so to speak that comes also goes away

and
is gone

Damp sheet pulled out from under a hip.
Moonlight, so much, not full, a quarter.
My hand in front of my face. Where to go?

In this room the sound of water, of breath.

In this dream you are you twenty years ago
getting up to pay for lunch

and I am me now thinking "My god,
what have I done?"

knowing
you will die in a day or two.

ENDINGS

There is a hollow. What was being in love
all about? A big book

lies open before me. I write my name. No.
Your name. Or was it our names?

Uncertainty has no place in romance.
Better to be let go. Not to know.

Thank god for the rain. The stillness
at its heart. Or my heart ... Il pleure ...

Often shortly after dying they come to her
in her dreams to say they are all right. I guess.

But me. I appear to her. Am I dead? Haunting the shower
every morning. Not soap. Not hot water. What?

There is an opening, an emptiness or gap. Why
do I want to say: "Cherry" or "Oak?"

That it is not rhetoric, nor a suddenness but a
quickening of moonlight if that can be imagined.

I forget the following. How it asks to be seen
in all its invisibility. Indivisibility? Is that it?

This loss. Indescribable. Constant. Like
the mind. Closer. An Elizabethan drama

at two in the morning. A grass-lined trough.
I don't feel alone yet am. Another life?

Bleeding somehow into this. A seam weakened.
Early. The last century. Great War.

"... that amazing Gewurztraminer you shared with us."
Domaine Weinbach. "It made him a part of the meal ..."

I turn out to be no Luther. For me, memorial. At most.
Bless the wine. It was only wine. Its own fragrant self.

Take a book off the shelf. There, that space.
I find myself napping hoping to fall into dream

as though that last fleeting touch is there, but gone
soon. Corner of my eye. Blue blazer, gray flannel

shock me. "I'm gone. Everything's okay. Tried to be
in touch earlier, but the lines were down." Blink

and you are gone. Where is the book that goes there?
Where the fullness I know persists?

Not a glass of wine. But water. Miraculous
as the breeze whose edge talks to me

of everything. Everyone but you. What
had I expected? Ghosts? Haunting details?

I don't know. Unless loss itself does away
with the previous itself. It must.

A stalk free from its roots floats
down the river. Seeing this, so would I.

Sad place. Not the people. Those I know.
Or don't. Their faces. Something bad.

Think of a Bollywood movie. An hour or so along.
When the unhappiness happens. No more

singing and dancing for at least another quarter hour.
Then there is an animal who bestows the gods' blessing.

Here I am. At what seems like
the end of everything. The next breath.

Poem. Thought. He said how sorry he was
for my loss. "Thomas." Dead. Gone.

Swallowed by doubt. Who wanders India.
Come back. I would love you. Care for you.

Something happened. It was blue
is about all I can say. Wait. There

were flowers. History isn't more than this.
Or this. To discover the story

all over again and to love it and not
the people in it.

It has come to this. A perfect afternoon.
In the shade of the porch. Slight movement

of air. Nowhere to go. Nowhere to come from.
That most extreme of isolations. The moment itself.

Now I weep for what? Can I even admit
these tears? What is gone? What to come?

The call that goes unanswered waits
like snow upon the air until it rains

and returns where? Damp ground
in a dry season? Are there corners

turned, and things just around them
unseen? No idea they were there.

Before the song. Before the path.
An open mouth. Ball of the foot.

This time tomorrow a public grief
hides in the arms of loud music.

Not one step further, neither left nor right.
Alone in the middle of that room.

Take a pillow and a blanket. Sleep
out on the porch. That much closer to

the incidence of rain. Naked. Maybe dream.
Nothing but the dawn is left me.

These are letters written forty years ago.
A light rain. Good. It's been so dry.

Where is that love. Still there. Ragged edges.
Brittle paper. Canceled checks. Stubs.

The moment the heart skips a beat
goes.

Gone. Perhaps I said. No more than a whiff
of sandalwood. Or smudge on the window pane

where someone pressed his face. Or hers. The scene
beyond lightly blurred off to one side. Just a bit.

Who was that? A familiar voice. Calling my name.
At the edge of sleep I wake. Not his. Whose?

Someone returns home unexpectedly. Not late.
But I've gone to bed. All but sound asleep.

That patch of day lilies I planted ten years ago
has begun to bloom. The time has come

for endings. A homelessness. Shopping cart.
Cardboard box.

Day itself. Free of anything but its blue.
Another few hours before sunlight falls

right here but beyond the hemlocks and
maples and poplars (I think they are)

it shines without hesitation. Nothing pauses
where I step then stand. My hands on my head.

It's here somewhere. I'll find it.
A scrap of paper.

Something I meant to say.
But wrote instead.

A couple sheets of white paper. Departures and arrivals.
Not lost. Maybe not even mislaid. This is the last time

I'll see you. Although I've got everything ready to go
apparently we don't leave until tomorrow. Sometimes

doesn't the psychopomp announce his final visit?
Here we are waylaid. Rather than beginning or ending.

Not the dog days yet
bright red leaves on the ground.

From the look of them
come from elsewhere. Some other time.

Tweed bent by no knee
nor cuff brushed . . .

They were talking about a suit. Whose?
What they said hard to hear

as though it came from another room
or another world.

OPEN WINDOW

Sudden flicker. Light, late afternoon. Bird. But
in that instance something expected. Some one
or thought. Gone. Here then not. The air
holds its shape a moment more. An instant
outlasts its own emptiness.
When my father died
his nurse opened the windows
"To let him go," she said.
In Chinese a hand reaches for the moon
to mean "have" or commonly "be."
To have to be. Or not. Grab
the moon or blot out its light.
There's no timing to these things.
Unless it's all timing. A beat impossible
to catch. The score appears in a dream
only to evaporate. Arms upraised.
A cat appears. Long lost. Almost forgot.
Where a music might redound
the sound of rain.

That pause in the day's occupation
comes. Loud music. Then thud. Silence.
Grandfather's hand (or an uncle's)
stirs up the cistern. This. And it's meant to be
the mind's confusion. Show me my heart.
I lie awake in the dark an hour
or two before dawn. Things
go through my mind. Thought
will wear them out. I hope.
Weren't those your last words to me:
"What do you think, Tom?"
A penny. A pansy. "Don't,"
I hear you say, "get too fancy."
This time I can find my way back.
Or wherever. I've done it before.
In another dream. How many before this.
Sandy-haired. Well-bred. Catholic family
(recent converts). He speaks to me in French.
(Is he?) Every word he says
betrays my understanding.
"I always saw you as the perfect couple,"
she said. That

second-person ambiguity amid the lush stuff and nonsense

coming at the end of something;

the beginning of something else.

The Beckoning Fair One.

That third who always joins the companions on the road.

The event opens the window

and comes through it. French sounds.

Are they words? Whose?

What proposes this? This asking.

Each minute lives in its dying.

Hear nothing to see.

Or remain. Remains.

The great K. N. Rao told me

"The moon dasha will be the best part of your life.

The mars dasha will be good. But none

better than the moon's." And

"Your sadhana goes well." Why not?

Have all that over with. Out from under

the waiting. Not the wanting. Not the weight.

Open book. No, open door. But why not?

Book. Door. Table. Chair. Blank

slate. Book. Over and over until there

is no over. The mind, the heart—whatever
holds—runs out.
My life rolls out there like a lawn.
Rolled? Now it's not so much the house,
its overlooking porch,
but the woods behind
that seem to me to be what's going on
or going forth.

OPEN DOOR

An open door. As though it were a policy
and everything you loved
the nation it governed. A dream
in the head of a long-haired kid
sitting at a table
with a cup of coffee
reading
a book
in Chinese.
To lie in wait. Lie in thought.
Along the fold of seeing what's going on
or not. Or not lifting
the slightest finger (sleight of hand).
Not wanting. Waiting.
What. For.
The window up. Did I say that?
There's been so much telling.
Not memory. Words. Their "how"

so that the right ... "distance" isn't it.
The right. Spaces. Openings.
A big white moon
suddenly there. (Which is the November one?
Can't remember.) A day
from full, caught in the tangled horizon
of bare branches. But not there
just now. A cloud hides it
from me. Something that was
isn't. A sky fire-engine red
over there.
A blank wall. A dream. Apparently in this one
no getting lost. Getting back is another matter.
Bottomless cup of black coffee. Isn't me
looking into it. Though I am and see
a sad end not mine. Letting go of everything.
I look at this photograph of you
and it alerts in me feelings for you
which are probably already there
and just tripped at this moment
but to what end? To say I miss you?

To say I want you back? When
the impossibility of that
stings.

This humility. Or is it helplessness?
Make it no secret.
What I am telling you.
If you hear it.
Tongue poised. Lips apart.
Puff of breath. God's name
flutters. Is gone. Here it was
and we were. Blink. No more.
Had I held on
it would have never been.
So near. The words. Speaking
in another room. What
are they saying? From the sound
they make they sound
like words said in an empty
room. Not to speak
because to speak

would be.

A bit of undigested potato. A dab
of mustard. I'd welcome
as this longing. To have
the elegant objectivity of
a Chinese poem
to explain ... No, rather
to comfort. To matter. How
to make a picture of
all that is taken
away?
An edge. Ocean? Land? Dark.
Here we are. Come this far. Feels
like you brought me. But. No.
Together the whole time until now.
That's the knife. No more beautiful than this
moment. Falling into place. I want but can't
deny. I go. You stay. Are gone.
I'm confused. Is this moment dependent upon the last?
Or is it the next? Neither feels like it to me.
Vast internal landscapes. Or seas. A pea-green boat.
Voyage. An occasional moment

devotes attention to what's at hand.
Lets it go. Seems to be enough
of whatever it takes.
What's today? The road to nowhere.
Ever diminishing particulars. Not
like loosing memories. Losing
the pause in the day's occupation.
A detail. An overlooked moment
recalled. That. That going.
Was going to leave it? Alone.
But turned. Decided no. Go on.
Unsure what was being avoided
then embraced—if that's the word.

Dream-like isn't the quality. Nor
fragmentary. Think of being lifted
then let go. Suddenly sometimes.
Other times somehow expected.
Since you died
(I wanted to say "Since you went away")
I've been living in a kind of Netherlands.
Flat, wet, and green. Though the light is gray

and thick and there are people on bicycles
all over the place. I don't speak the language.
It's not hard. It's not that I can't. I don't.
Something wrapped in a napkin
is all the time with me. Something yours.
Bread? A bit of cheese. Seemed sensible.
Simple. Or is it grief? Or that guilt let loose
when things end?

LAST POEM

Is this that? Let go. Sameness troubles me.
Table. Chair. Whatever. I know when I see it.

Things come and they go. Think of Langlois
and the Cinémathèque. Or the library at Alexandria.

These persistencies not of memory but the imagination.
Not what was lost. But that it was there.

The musical savant makes me wonder.
Is music simply tick-tock? Something

lacking ambiguity? Never fuzzy however
lush. Tone mashed upon tone like a platitude.

What does it mean when you dream a dream
where the place is not the place

and the people there not the people?
Is their anonymity a poem? A secret passage?

In a library. The book case swings open.
Here transgression is obscured and sleep awakes.

The girl is fourteen, maybe fifteen. Her brother, say, ten.
I catch sight of them. Think I know who they are.

Gone. Then they reappear. Did I see this the other day or
dream it. Same pair? How did I not see their utter beauty?

Not thinking. About stuff. Clear.
Plate-glass mind. My hesitation to mention it.

Or say loss of appetite.
And mean: "loss of soul."

Glitter of anticipation. Slant light. Momentary
car up the drive. But not. Breeze. Afternoon.

Can I get these few lines down? Before
he arrives?

Apparently the one thing they're not
telling us about desire is that

it is its own fulfillment whether we
stand in its way, deny, or flee.

Not sure what to do about it. The mention
of Pindar. Sun tangled in branches. Dogs barking.

A train. These edges symmetries disguised as
asymmetrical arise in gaps or lurk

in distracted moments to kick start the rhapsodic.
Did I eschew closure, deemed it folly

no less a fool for doing so. Stupidly thinking
metaphor was color. Blue blue. Red red.

Storm past. Still dark sky blends into
dusk. A rightness to it all.

But only now that my gut returns to normal.
Something set it wandering.

Suddenly all my soul in its care
washes and scrubs the poison without much

success. Then a sudden "aptness" draws
home the absence of well-being.

NEW POEM

I wake. It's hours before time
to get up.

I arrive at the airport long before
departure.

Another planet. All I've had is time.

What kind of poetry do you write?
Lyric. No. Rhapsodic. I don't know.

And it's about? I don't know.
Memory and loss. Boredom and deception.

A poetry of kind. About cows. A poetry
in kind. Kind poetry. Kind of.

Ars poetica.
Didn't think of that. When I said

I was writing a poem about writing
a poem she said:
Ars poetica.

I give myself airs: things to do.
Things done. Close my eyes
and I'm transported. Not far.
A room away. Almost a lifetime
folded into a split second

from here to there.
I thought I was ... Stop.
Don't say another word. Ars
poetica. How would you describe that?
He asked me. I wouldn't I said.

Is it grief? I return to? But let's take out
the "I." An other. No way I can know

what to talk about. Sit. Chat. The poem
a helplessness. Taken. "D'you come here often?"

Only to say: There it is.

Some time together.
Albeit a dream. And you had this dog with you.
Which makes sense. Don't ask me why.
The underworld I guess.

To talk with the dead. Is that
what the poem has left us?
To talk with the dead about desire.
If there were nothing

some part of it I'd want. Some part not.

Speak to me. Enough show. Now tell.
No more "palpable and mute" to describe the light.

Coin of the realm. Sticks and stones.
Cup half full. Sword dangling over my head.

But does the object come upon the verb?
The subject there from the beginning?

I can't look at these flame azalea in bloom
and not think:
Last

at least until those I love
and those I want to impress
have seen you.

Such is desire's currency.

Wait. That line. Those lines. A stanza
there this morning, almost a moment ago, drops
into a churning sea.

No loss. Release. Like a dream. Or a poem in a dream.
Only clarity remains. Clean window pane.
What was there

grasped a few minutes hasn't vanished but surrendered
color, released shape. Not unlike the lesson
lust teaches desire.

Odd how desire obstructs its object. Or
did I mean "obliterates?"

Wanting the chocolate cake. Having
the chocolate cake. Two different things

there is hardly ever at their specific moment
time to see they aren't the same.

All dressed up. Nowhere
to go.

All technology heads for
the useless.

I'd've thought Heidegger
saw that.

Or did he? The other way round.
Through the telescope
backwards.

Once or when the poem
was a bright shiny thing, think
what it could or would do . . .

The logical conclusion then
is that

everything that goes
wants to be
its place holder.

NEPENTHE

*No doubt there were prophets in Pompeii who warned of the
dangers of living under volcanoes, but it is doubtful whether
even the pessimists among them actually expected the total
and definitive obliteration of the city.* ERIC HOBSBAWN

My son eats his lunch. Takes a picture
and emails me it like the guy I had
sex with a couple weeks ago sent
a friend in the City live details of
our realizing each other.

Constance Garnett sits in her garden
and scribbles *War & Peace* into English.
I brought the Great Crystal. Who
can lift it much less look into it? I emptied
your ashes into the beck. The river. The sea.

Don't speak. The still point is lost to words.
My head in your hands finds it in silence.